Soul Toolbox

How to Include Your Soul in Healing Trauma

By
Victoria McGee, M.A.

©2022

All rights reserved. No part of this publication may be reproduced, distributed, or transmitted in any form or by any means, including photocopying, recording, or other electronic or mechanical methods, without the prior written permission of the publisher, except in the case of brief quotations embodied in critical reviews and certain other noncommercial uses permitted by copyright law. For permission requests, contact the author through victoriamcgee.com.

Copyright 2022 by Victoria McGee

Ordering Information:
For details, contact mcgeepublications@yahoo.com

Print ISBN: 978-0-9755629-3-2
eBook ISBN: 978-0-9755629-4-9

Printed in the United States of America on SFI Certified paper.

First Edition

INTRODUCTION

As the people of the world seem to be in a constant cycle of trauma and healing, I was moved to offer something simple; a balm for the spirit. A Trauma Toolbox is for fellow humans who have experienced any type of trauma, and is designed to augment and complement therapeutic treatment with a focus on the soul. Nothing can replace or compare to good, solid, therapy regarding trauma, and there are so many effective modalities available now. My hope is that you, the reader, have found the right one for you.

A Trauma Toolbox is a daily practice, a way to bring your soul into your healing process and focus your mind and spirit each day toward healing. As trauma survivors, it's important to acknowledge that our soul is also wounded. We may be in traditional therapy, physical therapy, whatever it takes to heal the unimaginable; integrating soul work into these therapies will only bring deeper healing and strengthen our ability to move forward.

This simple toolbox follows the English alphabet, with a word, a thought, to be read and contemplated each day. Each thought is surrounded by quotes from healers and thought-leaders on the subjects of trauma and healing, faith and grace. Each daily thought includes a meditation with an intention to carry through the day. Each page concludes with a journal prompt if you are a person who gains insight through journaling.

So, I offer 26 days or 26 ways to include your soul in healing trauma. It's a toolbox to use for self-compassion, growth, and to enhance the healing of your mind and body. What you can build with this toolbox (in tandem with traditional therapy) is a wholly healed human. No small task. For me, the soul component was critical in my own healing of trauma. It helped me find a forgiveness beyond forgiveness. It helped me rebuild my faith in myself, my fellow humans, and God. Rebuilding this faith is a gift to yourself that *only you can experience*. No one can give this to you, all wrapped up in a pretty package. You have to seek it out, practice it, and acknowledge your progress along the way.

Many others have walked this journey before us. They give us hope - and a blueprint! I learned from them, and hope to pass along as much as I understand – so far. I'm still learning, still growing, still healing. I hope this toolbox provides you a structured yet spiritual way to include your beloved soul in healing trauma. Let's hold hands and begin.

Victoria McGee
June 2022

TABLE OF CONTENTS

SECTIONS	PAGE #
1. ALLOW	1
2. BREATHE	3
3. COURAGE	7
4. DIVINE	11
5. ENDURE	15
6. FORGIVE	19
7. GRIEF	23
8. HONOR	27
9. INTEGRATE	31
10. JOURNAL	35
11. KNOWLEDGE	39
12. LISTEN	43
13. MINDFULNESS	47
14. NATURE	51
15. OWN IT	55
16. POWER	59
17. QUIET	63
18. RITUAL	67
19. SELF-COMPASSION	71
20. TRUST	75
21. UNBREAKABLE	79

22. VISION	83
23. WISDOM	87
24. (E)XERCISE	91
25. YES	95
26. ZEN	99

For my sister.

A

ALLOW

"Healing does not mean going back to the way things were before, but rather allowing what is now to move us closer to God."
~ Ram Dass

Often, when we think about healing from trauma, we have a strong desire to feel like we did before we experienced trauma. It's like wanting psychic surgery to remove the memories and the residual stress and anxiety, even as we know that is not possible. However, the more we want it taken away, the longer it takes to heal.

To allow means that just for today, just for this moment, we allow whatever we're feeling to be okay. We try not to judge it, but simply notice it, and *allow* it. We allow where we are in our healing process to be the perfect place, not desiring to be better quicker, but trusting that even on the days we may not feel it, healing is happening. We allow space for the healing, not in spite of our feelings today, but welcoming all of them as part of the process.

Meditation:

Today I allow my healing process to be whatever it is, without judgment. I allow my feelings to be present and to feel them fully, without judgment. I allow myself to sit with the current state of my mind, body, and soul, without judgment. I allow myself to be in my current stage of healing – I rest in it – I place my hand on my heart, and with compassion for myself, I remind myself that I am capable of allowing myself to feel and to heal.

Today, I allow my healing process to be whatever it is, without judgment.

"We, like the Mother of the World, become the compassionate presence that can hold, with tenderness, the rising and passing waves of suffering." ~ Tara Brach

Journal prompt: What are some areas of resistance in my healing journey? Where could I focus the energy of allowing?

B

BREATHE

"Breath is the bridge which connects life to consciousness, which unites your body to your thoughts. Whenever your mind becomes scattered, use your breath as the means to take hold of your mind again."
~ Thich Nhat Hanh

The importance of learning to breathe, and regulating our breath, whether in meditation or simple relaxation techniques, cannot be overstated when it comes to healing trauma. The benefits of mastering the breath have been scientifically documented. The beneficial effect on our mind and nervous system is measurable, and the best part is, it's free.

According to Harvard Health, when we shallow breathe, the lower part of our lungs never gets their full share of oxygenated air. This can leave us feeling short of breath and anxious. This is why taking deeper breaths often will relax us right away. Our lower lungs receive oxygen and no longer panic that there isn't enough breath for us to survive. When we blend deep breathing with relaxing music, imagery or a mantra of some kind, the benefits are even greater.

As we recover from trauma, we practice regulating our breath as it helps us regulate our nervous system. We learn we are not at the mercy of outside forces that might make us tense, angry, or scattered. We empower ourselves with the ability to take charge of our breath, filling our lungs completely, noticing our capacity to take care of ourselves.

The 4–square breathing method is helpful for many people. It is simple and you can do it anywhere. Inhale deeply to a count of four, hold your breath for a count of four, exhale for a count of four, and hold again for a count of four before inhaling again. Think of nothing but counting the breath, repeat until you feel calm.

Meditation:

Today I practice breathing with intent. I set aside time to sit and simply notice my breath. I fill my lungs as deeply as I can with oxygen, observing how my diaphragm supports my lungs. Like water, breath is vital for survival, and I recognize that, for me, breath is a balm for healing trauma. I am grateful for this tool, and I commit to use it when I am triggered, or anxious, or scattered. I inhale Divine healing and peace, and exhale tension and fear.

Today, I recognize that I am capable of using my own breath as a tool of calm.

"Wherever we are, we can take a deep breath, feel our body, open our senses, and step outside the endless stories of the mind."
~ Jack Kornfeld

Journal prompt: Practice a breathing technique. Write about how your body felt, and how you felt in your body, before and after the breathing practice.

C

COURAGE

"Courage doesn't always roar. Sometimes courage is the quiet voice at the end of the day that says 'I will try again tomorrow.'"
~ Mary Anne Radmacher

Physical healing requires courage, but our bodies come wired to heal whenever a wound occurs. Not so with mental, emotional, or spiritual healing. These require tremendous courage and a conscious resolve we don't always feel capable of. Like physical therapy for recovery from physical wounds, trauma recovery requires regular attention, stretching our minds and hearts, and facing our psychic wounds full on with compassion and the determination to heal.

Healing trauma requires the courage to not only recognize our wounds, explore and integrate the tools it takes to be wholly functional again, but also face the fact that this wound is now part of us, and how we carry it will determine much of our life going forward. It also requires courage to seek and ask for help, to move on when the help isn't quite right, and to let certain people and places fall away that no longer serve our highest good.

Healing isn't easy, but it is necessary, and the courage to do it can come from many places! Look for support from God, friends, therapists, and support groups. All who have healed trauma will tell you it took tremendous courage, so remember that you are not alone. You are not alone.

Meditation:

Today I take time to acknowledge that the journey I am on requires courage, perhaps more courage than has ever been required of me. I close my eyes and place my hand on my belly, knowing that I have reserves of strength within to draw upon. I discover that my desire to heal is stronger than the fear of facing my trauma, for I know my life will be fuller and more balanced for having healed this wound.

Today, I give my fear to God, filling my breath, lungs and belly with courage and strength, recognizing that these powerful attributes already dwell within me.

"You're not a victim for sharing your story, you are a survivor setting the world on fire with your truth. And you never know who needs your light, your warmth, and raging courage." ~ Alex Elle

Journal prompt: Write about someone whose courage you admire. Draw parallels between their courageous path and your own.

D

DIVINE

"I looked in temples, churches, and mosques. But I found the Divine within my heart." ~ Rumi

The Divine, God, Yahweh, the Universe, whatever you believe, whatever brings you comfort, is an integral and necessary part of healing from trauma. In addition to therapy (a mental and emotional journey), engaging your soul in healing trauma is the spiritual part of your journey that will provide a framework for your perception of what you've experienced and how you might choose to move forward.

We often wonder why this trauma occurred. It occurred because we are living a human life, and sometimes terrible things happen. This quote from author Jennifer Worth is particularly helpful when we start to question why: "God is not in the event. God is in the response to the event." We cannot in this life understand why certain things happen, but we can engage the Divine in responding to what happened.

Prayer and meditation are your direct links to the Divine. Opening this channel will provide you with a GPS system for navigating your healing. Let God guide your response to this event. Let the Divine hold you as you take this healing journey. Rely on, lean on, and trust the Universe. Trust the Divine within yourself. You don't need to have all the strength for the journey; God will carry your burden if you will give it.

Meditation:

Today, I rely on the Divine to guide my healing. I ask for balm for my soul, for my wounded heart and mind. I relax into the arms of God, knowing I will be given guidance when to work hard for my healing, and when to rest. I accept God's grace and love, surrendering into God's strength, knowing I'm not doing this alone.

Today, I give my healing process to the Divine, resting in the presence of God, trusting that healing is happening and bowing my head in gratitude.

> *"When you enter a place of stillness, you awaken the divinity within you."* ~ Peggy Sealfon

Journal prompt: Investigate what the Divine means to you. How has your vision of God changed throughout your life? Did your experience of trauma change your relationship with God?

E

ENDURE

"The most authentic thing about us is our capacity to create, to overcome, to endure, to transform, to love and to be greater than our suffering." ~ Ben Okri

You will endure. You will survive this. You will overcome trauma. Some days that may sound impossible, or not even like something you want to or can do. It sounds daunting. But I assure you the human spirit can prevail.

We all have within us a strong survival instinct. It sparks our flight, fight, or freeze reaction, programmed deep within our brains to keep us alive. It can also be called upon when we are spiraling down into depression, lying awake with anxiety, or gripped with fear spawned by memory. Many people find there are moments in trauma recovery when it feels too hard, or times we don't feel capable of doing the work. We may feel resentful we even have to do the work – we didn't ask to be a trauma survivor, after all.

But those are the times we need to reach down to that survival instinct. We must tell ourselves we will not let this defeat us.

It's often helpful to look to others who have survived trauma, overcome it, and endured in spite of it. There are many examples of famous people, but you undoubtedly know someone in your own life who was tested and who survived, endured, and rose above. Look at their resilience and know this ability lives in you as well. Turn your despair over to God. Let God transmute your overwhelm, lighting a small spark inside you – a spark of knowledge, a fire of survival, an Olympic flame of enduring.

Meditation:

Today, I rest in the sure knowledge that I will endure. I know there is a reason I am alive, and that I am here for reasons I can't even imagine yet. In my quiet space, I reach to that part of me that is driven to survive. I feel my drive to endure grow within me and fill my inner being with the glow of life. I bask in this enduring warmth and feel it in every part of me. I want to live, and live fully.

Today, I commit to enduring. I will continue, and take one step forward toward healing each day, relying on the strength and guidance of Divine Love.

> *"That you are here – that life exists and identity,*
> *That the powerful play goes on,*
> *and you may contribute a verse."* ~ Walt Whitman

Journal prompt: Write about a time in the future. See that you have endured and healed trauma. Describe what you see.

F

FORGIVE

"Forgiveness is not about letting someone off the hook for their actions, but freeing ourselves of negative energies that bind us to them."
~ Satsuki Shibuya

Forgiveness is as necessary and intrinsic to healing from trauma as physical therapy is to healing an injury. It needs to be done daily, and in a manner that doesn't hurt you, but stretches you. Forgiveness also doesn't need to be rushed. When it is time, you feel it. And when you forgive, you will feel lighter. Forgiveness is the skeleton key that unlocks the shackles of fear and rage that we carry around.

Forgiveness is very much a process, as is any type of healing. Do as much as you can, when you can. And know that is enough. Forgiving isn't easy. It takes courage and faith of a rare kind. When you're ready, angels will surround you, lift you up, and imbue you with everything you need.

There is a part of us that thinks forgiveness is too difficult where trauma is involved, that we are letting someone off the hook. But it will be impossible to have true peace (and you will actually carry the trauma longer) if you do not find a way to forgive. Do you want to chain yourself to this trauma forever? Of course not. So you forgive. You do it for yourself, not for them.

So how do we get to forgiveness? Not by yourself. Ask God for help. And ask again. And when you think you're done, ask again. It never happens all at once, but in stages, so learn to recognize when you're ready to forgive just a little bit more. And keep chipping away at it. *You'll know* when the wound is completely healed.

Meditation:

Today, I take a step forward in forgiveness. I recognize that I am healing from trauma, and that forgiveness is one component of this process. I try to identify a way in to forgiveness today. Perhaps it is compassion for what may have caused another person's behavior, such as pain or anger or desperation. Perhaps it is recognizing that forces larger than myself or another person were at work, as in war.

Today, I forgive so I may release this poison from my heart. Today, I forgive so I may move forward lighter in my soul. Today, I forgive for my own peace.

"Forgive others not because they deserve forgiveness, but because you deserve peace."
~ Jonathan Lockwood Hule

Journal prompt: Explore your relationship with forgiveness. Do you find it easy or difficult? What are your fears and feelings around forgiving others?

G

GRIEF

"Grief is in two parts. The first is loss. The second is the remaking of life." ~ Anne Roiphe

With trauma often comes grief. Sometimes a loss is trauma itself. Sometimes we grieve the person we were before trauma touched our lives. Either way, grief is a component of trauma that you will feel and, in time, integrate.

As with any loss, your grief surrounding trauma is completely appropriate. You may be mourning a loss of innocence, a loss of the feeling of safety, or the loss of feeling care-free in the world. These are not everyday losses and should not be treated as such. Just as joy is an appropriate response to good news, grief can be an appropriate response to trauma. If nothing else, we often simply mourn the fact that trauma has touched our lives and we will never be the same.

Allow yourself to feel the grief associated with trauma. Feel deeply the losses surrounding what you have been through. If you do not take some time to grieve, the sorrow will rise up in the future. Like a whale coming up for air, it cannot stay submerged forever. The sorrow is there, so rather than avoid it, let it be acknowledged, felt, and given compassion, so it may be released. Then, comfort yourself in the knowledge that grief does lessen over time, and know that the loss you feel is being alchemized into strength, wisdom, and peace as you heal.

Meditation:

Today, I allow myself to grieve, not to wallow in sorrow, but to deeply acknowledge the losses I have endured. I create a safe space for these feelings, a container for them, and trust myself to feel hard feelings without getting lost in them. I anchor myself in the here and now, and then allow the grief to come. I am safe, I am grieving, I am healing, and I am where I need to be, doing what I need to be doing.

Today, I trust the Universe to guide me into grief and out again. I trust myself to heal as much as I can today, and relax in knowing whatever it is, is enough.

*"The darker the night, the brighter the stars,
The deeper the grief, the closer to God."*
~ Fyodor Dostoevsky

Journal prompt: What loss do you grieve? Is this loss connected to trauma, or a trauma itself? What is the relationship between trauma and grief in your life?

H

HONOR

"Pull over to the side of the journey and look how far you've come."
~ Danielle LaPorte

It's such a full-time job to heal, isn't it? Sometimes we feel like Sisyphus, eternally pushing a rock up this hill that others call everyday life. And, like a full-time job, it's important that we take breaks, periods of rest, and honor ourselves for our hard work.

Just as no one can walk this path for you, no one can acknowledge the work you've done either. Only you know the breathing, the reading, the therapy, the nights of constant praying, of turning it over to God again and again and again. Only you know - and God. The Divine is always looking for opportunities for us to heal more **and** to acknowledge us when we do. Think of the times when the opportunities to heal would lessen so you could catch your breath and just live. Similarly, there are times when the opportunities intensify because the next phase of healing needs to occur in order to move forward.

When we can pause to catch our breath in the healing process, we need to take a moment and truly see how far we've come. Like a butterfly that has gone through so much to emerge, pause and appreciate the transformation taking place. When we stop to admire a butterfly, it's not just their beauty we're in awe of; it's the miraculous metamorphosis from crawling caterpillar to winged wonder. As we crawl out of trauma, let us remember to take time to honor the strength, courage, and faith it takes to walk this journey, and take rest.

Meditation:

Today, I pause to acknowledge the hard healing work I have done. I am on a journey that is not for the faint-hearted, yet I face it most days with courage and even optimism that I am healing.

I place my hand on my heart and offer myself compassion for all I've been through, and tenderness for the still-bruised places inside me. I ask the Divine to continue to hold me up and fill me with strength and grace, and help me find opportunities to celebrate the small victories that only **we** know about.

Today, I honor myself! I honor my grit, my steadfastness, my relentless need to heal, and I rest, amazed and grateful at where I am on this journey.

"There's time for healing and time for rest. Don't get so caught up in healing that you forget to acknowledge all the progress you've made."
~ Ash Alves

Journal prompt: What are the ways you acknowledge your hard healing work? If you don't do it enough, what are ways you could honor yourself for this? Write out a plan for regularly rewarding your healing progress.

I

INTEGRATE

"Your healing will take you someplace new, someplace whole, someplace where your trauma and your healing integrate to create wisdom and peace." ~ Liz Milani

As we travel a healing path, we will integrate what we are learning along the way. Sometimes this happens naturally, sometimes we can help it along. Healing trauma involves all aspects of our humanness. We are called upon to heal our body, our mind, our heart *and* our spirit on this journey.

Remember learning vocabulary words? We learned the individual words and their meaning, and then, at some point, would stumble upon them in reading. And our mind would say, "Ah! I know this word!" We first gained the knowledge, then we were able to integrate it into our experience. So it is with healing trauma. We learn individual lessons, such as courage, boundaries, strength, or forgiveness, and are then given opportunities in life to use those lessons, to integrate them into our daily life. We find that as we learn, change takes place. We are not the person we were before – perhaps we are stronger, more compassionate, or less fearful. As we grow in the confidence of healing, we take a firmer stance with the world. Our feet are more firmly planted. We integrate our well-earned healing into everyday existence. We do this through practice, meditation, prayer, self-reflection and perhaps helping others.

Like physical therapy, daily practice, staying present, working the muscles of our heart and spirit will bring about an integration of ourselves as wholly healed.

Meditation:

Today I ask God to show me where I am already healed and how I might integrate that learning. I accept that my healing journey is ongoing, but rather than feel fatigued by this, I feel energized and encouraged, knowing that I am integrating learning that I could not have achieved any other way. I ask that this learning result in compassion, both for myself and others, that my heart opens wide to offer love to myself, and those around me. I am grateful, and I know the integration of this learning will make me a fuller, deeper, more whole person.

Today I recognize the areas in my life where I have changed and grown as a result of the struggle to heal this trauma, and I see it now as my ability to integrate profound lessons.

"Becoming integrated and whole is the spiritual path. The body is your vehicle. Your job is to learn about yourself from your experiences and change yourself. This is spiritual growth."
~ Gary Zukav

Journal prompt: Reflect on pieces of knowledge you've acquired and integrated into daily life. Examine the ways you might be using some piece of wisdom each day without consciously thinking about it. Describe ways you might integrate the wisdom gained through healing trauma.

J

JOURNAL

"I can shake off everything as I write; my sorrows disappear, my courage is reborn." ~ Anne Frank

One way to help process all the emotions surrounding trauma is by journaling. If you haven't ever tried it, perhaps today is the day. Some people find it easy to pour their thoughts and feelings out onto the page. For others, it's not as easy and you may find it difficult to get started. There are websites and books offering journal prompts, which can be extremely helpful. You can always start by simply answering a simple question; "How do I feel today?" or "What feels difficult today?" or "What went well today?"

Why journal? Journaling has been scientifically shown to help people sort out their emotions and gain clarity of their thoughts. It even has physical benefits such as lowering blood pressure and boosting the immune system! Trauma can lead to anxiety and chaotic feelings. James Pennebaker, a journaling researcher at UT Austin, says, "By writing, you put some structure and organization to those anxious feelings. It helps you to get past them."

Journaling is an ingenious and simple way to help integrate your experience by engaging the mind and the heart, the left brain and the right brain. The act of putting pen to paper engages the logical mind, and helps the emotions organize themselves into manageable pieces of thought. It speeds the integration of your experience, and ignites deeper healing. It is also a private process, so you are free to write, draw, or scribble whatever you want without judgment. Just let come whatever needs to come.

Meditation:

Today, I give myself time to write. I set an intention to write often, especially when I need clarity in my thoughts and feelings, or to process a therapy session. I trust the process will guide me to insights and further healing. I ask God and my higher self to guide my pen and allow the words to flow for my highest good.

Today, I write what needs to be released. I join my heart and mind in a process of healing through journaling. I give myself over to this practice and I am grateful.

"In the journal I do not just express myself more openly than I could to any person: I create myself." ~ Susan Sontag

Journal prompt: What needs to be released? What needs to be said? Don't hold back, simply let it flow and let it go!

K

KNOWLEDGE

"Hardships often prepare ordinary people for an extraordinary destiny." ~ C.S. Lewis

If we are to rise above our trauma, we eventually must begin to recognize the strengths we can gain through surviving and healing trauma. One of these is knowledge. Through trauma, we gain knowledge we could not have found any other way. This is when we experience post-traumatic growth, a very real phenomenon.

What knowledge have you gained as a result of surviving and healing trauma? For many, it is a stronger sense of self, perhaps a commitment to better boundaries, and a resilience that commands we see ourselves with respect and awe for what we have lived through, and how we have handled it. Even if you don't see it every day, you will see it more frequently as you heal. They say time heals all wounds, and time also gives us perspective on the knowledge those wounds may have provided us.

Trauma brings about change. We may feel we're not the same person, we don't have the same light in our eyes. But we have a different light. We have the light of a deeper person, a person who now has the tools of knowledge and wisdom to keep healing, and continue growing.

Meditation:

Today, I endeavor to appreciate the knowledge I have gained through trauma work. I examine areas of my life that have changed and I see now how my healing has informed that change. I ask God to show me the knowledge I have already earned, and ask that I be given more, when I am ready for it. I do not take this knowledge lightly, as it is hard-won, and I commit to cherish and be grateful for it.

Today, I acknowledge my post-traumatic growth. I know I have become a deeper person, and I know my deep healing and deep regard for this knowledge is a balm for my soul.

> *"The knowledge that you have emerged wiser and stronger from setbacks means that you are, ever after, secure in your ability to survive."* ~ J.K. Rowling

Journal prompt: Make a list of ways you have expanded in self-knowledge while healing trauma.

L

LISTEN

"When you listen with your soul, you come into rhythm and unity with the music of the universe." ~ John O'Donohue

As we heal, we become more and more aware how important it is to create time to listen to our hearts and souls. The world is full of distraction and noise. It is always easy to find something to fill a silence or distract our thoughts. Sometimes, at certain stages of healing, distraction serves a purpose. But as we deepen into healing, carving out time for meditation, prayer and silent time with Spirit is essential.

Deep listening doesn't have to happen during a dedicated meditation time. We can utilize walking meditation, spend time in nature, or simply focus in on a single moment and really listen to the environment. During dedicated meditation and prayer, attempt to keep your mind from wandering, trying instead to empty your mind of expectation and questions. When you truly listen with an open heart, you will find yourself cradled in the safety and dynamic love of the Universe. The poet Rumi said, "There is a voice that doesn't use words. Listen." The comfort you receive will be wordless, but you will recognize it as something you've been longing for all along.

Meditation:

Today, I focus on listening. When distraction calls me, and my thoughts want to constantly look outside myself for relief, I will instead look within. I allow myself to be in silence, even briefly, and truly listen to my heart and soul. I breathe within this space and ask to hear the music of the universe. All I need is within me.

Today, I listen to Silence. Today, I listen to Spirit. Today, I listen to Source.

"In solitude, there is healing. Speak to your soul. Listen to your heart. Sometimes in the absence of noise we find the answers." ~ Dodinsky

Journal prompt: After meditation, write about your experience listening to your heart and soul. Could you discern soul thoughts from mind thoughts? How did you feel before and after?

M

MINDFULNESS

"Mindfulness is a pause – the space between stimulus and response: that's where choice lies."
~ Tara Brach

The practice of mindfulness is one of the most important tools we can carry in our toolbox. It is a skill that, once learned, can be used to return us to peace of mind again and again. Mindfulness is a form of meditation, a mental exercise wherein we focus completely on the present moment. Whatever you are doing, you do it with complete awareness, whether you are making a bed, taking a shower, or preparing a meal. You work with your mind to keep it focused only on what is happening *right now*. In a state of mindfulness, our thoughts are not able to create anxiety by worrying about the future, or depression by dwelling on the past.

When our thoughts feel scattered and chaotic, or when they have flown, unharnessed, in a direction that causes un-ease, mindfulness practice can help us rein in these thoughts and feel the gift of conscious presence. All that is actually happening is what is before you. Anything in the past is not happening right now. Anything in the future has not happened yet. The present moment is all that exists. Practicing mindfulness means we have choice and control over our thoughts, a powerful and practical tool for all survivors of trauma. Having control of our thoughts begins to restore our ability to feel in control again in life.

Meditation:

Today, I will practice staying in the present moment as it occurs. I will attempt to stay mindful in every situation, conversation or task I engage in. When I am tempted to distract my mind with worry about the future or regret about the past, I will bring my awareness back to what is happening right now and breathe into the present moment.

Today, I practice mindfulness and feel the gift of true awareness. In a changing world, I use this tool to ground myself in conscious presence and choose to be here now. I give myself fully only to this moment.

"Mindfulness helps us get better at seeing the difference between what is happening and the stories we tell ourselves about what is happening." ~ Sharon Salzberg

Journal prompt: Write about the times it is difficult to harness your thoughts. Are you spinning in the past or the future? Come up with a phrase you can tell yourself when you need a mindful moment.

N

NATURE

*"I go to nature to be soothed and healed,
and to have my senses put in order."*
~ John Burroughs

Nature has long been seen as a place to heal and restore our souls. The more humans have moved to indoor lifestyles, the more our psyches have suffered for lack of connection to the natural world. To help heal our trauma, it is beneficial to find some way to connect to nature. It reminds us of the constancy of the earth and the water, and also reminds us that when there is change, either through seasons or catastrophe, nature (of which we are a part) survives and is resilient.

Although ancient peoples knew the healing properties of the earth, science is now proving what our ancestral instinct has always felt. Research has shown that time in nature can lower blood pressure, reduce nervous system arousal, help balance immune system function, improve mood and reduce anxiety. Quite an abundance of healing balm at no charge! Even if you can't take a walk in the woods or on a beach, spending time in a park, sitting under a tree, bonding with animals, or gardening on an apartment patio can provide the same benefits. As you take good care of yourself, be sure to schedule in some time for nature to nourish you.

Meditation:

Today, I commit to spend time in the natural world. I ask Mother Earth to fill me with her gifts; constancy, adaptability, and resilience. I accept these gifts and internalize them, knowing they represent a strength that is already part of me, I need only to tap into it. I am grateful for the gifts of nature and I allow myself to sink into and become one with nature, relaxing in the safety of her power and embrace.

Today, I spend time in nature. I breathe in the earth and breathe out anxiety. I ground myself and feel supported and nourished by Mother Earth. Today, nature is my remedy.

> *"Sit long in Nature, and after a while she'll sit within you. Let her take away your name, your history, and everything on your to-do list. Let her mess up your hair, dirty your feet, and awaken to your inner poetry."* ~ Tanya Markul

Journal prompt: Take your notebook and pen outside and write about what you see. Write about how it makes you feel. Breathe it in and write it out.

O

OWN IT

"Owning our story and loving ourselves through that process is the bravest thing that we'll ever do." ~ Brene Brown

Surviving and healing trauma involves the difficult task of owning it. This is vastly different from owning *up* to something as trauma is not something we caused. Rather, owning it refers to taking the hard journey of accepting that you are a survivor of trauma, and that it will forever be part of you. It's not a journey you asked for, and there is grief in that, profound grief for a part of us that is gone, perhaps an innocent or vulnerable part. There is also anger that must be felt and acknowledged and processed. But out beyond that, owning it means accepting that you are changed, you are practicing self-compassion, and you are actively engaged in the responsibility of your healing.

Acceptance, owning it, is key to your complete healing. Without it, we suffer under a cloud of denial, obscuring the light available to us. Without it, we may get stuck in victimhood, never knowing the power available in standing in our truth and owning where we have been. When we can own our journey, integrate the changes it has brought and keep putting one foot in front of the other on our healing path, it becomes possible to one day become a vehicle and a catalyst for healing others.

Meditation:

Today, I practice total acceptance of the trauma I have survived. I acknowledge that, having happened, it is forever part of me. As I practice self-compassion and loving myself today, I realize I must love all parts of me, even this. It all belongs and makes up who I am. I cannot cut this part out of my life or memory, nor would I want to, as it is a tool I choose to utilize for personal and spiritual growth. I recognize it for what it is - a foothold for my ability to stand in my own power. I own this trauma, as much as I own the healing afterward.

Today, I commit to owning all parts of myself, loving all parts of myself, and nourishing myself with healing thoughts and habits. I surrender my healing to God as I accept my path and find gratitude for it.

"Whatever happens to you belongs to you. Make it yours. Feed it to yourself even if it feels impossible to swallow. Let it nurture you, because it will." ~ Cheryl Strayed

Journal prompt: How does it feel to truly own your journey? Are you embracing it or resisting it? What might it look like if you fully embrace it?

P

POWER

"Stop giving your power away and trust that your feelings are in fact expressions of the deepest truths."
~ Neale Donald Walsch

Often the circumstances of trauma leave us feeling powerless. It is important to find ways to reclaim our personal power so that whatever we are trying to heal feels manageable and we feel capable of the work. When we allow the trauma to cripple us, becoming stuck in suffering, we give away our power. Of course, when trauma is fresh, we are often fragile and personal power is elusive. But as we begin to heal, it is important information to notice *when* we are triggered and how those triggers affect our personal power. As we heal and identify triggers, they can become the perfect catalyst for learning how and when to not give our power away.

Using the tools we are acquiring; breathing, courage, and mindfulness, we can meet triggers and consciously decide to stand firm in our own power. We stay in the present moment, breathe slowly and deeply, and shift focus to our stance, grounding in our power, relaxing into safety, breathing in calm, breathing out fear. Herein lies our power. Our power also comes from the healing action we can take for ourselves every day: good therapy, soothing forms of art, finding laughter, helping others, praying. We are truly spiritual warriors, healing that which can seem impossible, but we are doing it.

Meditation:

Today, I recognize and send love to those parts of me that feel fragile or hopeless. I breathe into these spaces – breathing in calm, breathing out anxiety, breathing in hope, breathing out despair, breathing in power, breathing out fear. As I breathe, I take up the shield of protecting my personal power. I vow to not give away this power to memories or triggers or people who would seek to keep me stuck. I hold onto the present moment and breathe.

Today, my Power is available to me as I practice igniting the spark I carry within me. I ask the Divine to replenish my power when I forget, and to shore me up when the foundation of my healing structure is shaken by the storms of daily life. I ask God's power to be fused with my own this day.

> *"You deserve peace, love, happiness and all that your heart desires. Don't let anyone control your life and take away those things."* ~
> Sonya Parker

Journal prompt: Describe a situation where you felt in power, fully in control and at peace. What were the circumstances? What did it feel like in your body? Reflect on ways to apply this practice to other situations.

Q

QUIET

"We need quiet time to examine our lives openly and honestly – spending quiet time alone gives your mind an opportunity to renew itself and create order." ~ Susan L. Taylor

One of the best tools for healing the mind and heart and soul is quiet time. As survivors of trauma, we may perhaps turn to noise and bustle as a distraction from thoughts that may haunt us from time to time, or to not feel alone. However, as all great spiritual teachers have reminded us throughout time, what we seek we already know within. Ram Dass said, "The quieter you become, the more you can hear." Maya Angelou also advised, "Listen to yourself, and in that quietude, you might hear the voice of God."

Compare your inner self to your physical body. If you feed it all day long, nonstop, it will grow unhealthy, even toxic. Likewise, a constant diet of outer stimuli is damaging to our mind and soul. Think about what you feed your mind, heart, and soul throughout the day. Carving out quiet time is a gift to the parts of our psyche that need calm nurturing, the parts that long to listen to inner guidance, and the parts that pine for communion with the Divine. We all go through times in our lives when being alone in the quiet with our own thoughts can actually be quite frightening. That is normal, especially in trauma recovery. Still, finding some moments of quiet, even a minute or two to start, will begin to build neurons of safety and self-compassion in our mind that actually repair fear and anxiety. Over time, you will form a solid foundation out of the quiet that can handle anything you bring to it. If a quiet place is difficult to come by, or total silence is not comfortable, try ambient music, headphones, anything you need to reach that place within is appropriate.

Meditation:

Today, I allow myself time to be in a quiet place. I honor myself by carving out a time and place and I dedicate it to quieting my soul. I let go of outer chaos, leaving it behind as I enter a realm of pause and peace. I befriend myself and relish this time of joining with the consciousness that exists only in quiet space.

Today, I relax in quiet. Today, I breathe into the quiet. Today, I rest in quiet as I allow it to envelop me in warmth, spiritual communion, and self-compassion. I am safe. I am quiet.

> *"Silence is essential. We need silence, just as much as we need air, just as much as plants need light. If our minds are crowded with words and thoughts, there is no space for us."*
> ~ Thich Nhat Hanh

Journal prompt: How do you feel about quiet time with yourself? Do you avoid it or relish it? Do you never have enough or is it too much? Write a mantra for yourself to use in quiet meditation.

R

RITUAL

"Ritual cuts through and operates on everything besides the 'head' level." ~ Aiden Kelly

When we seek comfort, we can often find it in ritual. A ritual doesn't have to be fancy, or religious, or complicated. It can be as simple as taking your morning coffee or tea in the same spot every day, breathing and centering. It can include yoga, meditation, prayer, exercise – anything that you do regularly and that you can rely on. There is a reason rituals are passed down within families, cultures, and religions. A ritual can be an anchor, a way to hold fast to what is known when the unknown presents a challenge in our lives.

In this world, we must often deal with unexpected turmoil. It can be a small thing that didn't turn out like we planned, or it can encompass overwhelming grief and loss. Developing and practicing a daily ritual gives us solid ground to fall back on in times of stress. Whatever is going on around us, when we fall into ritual there is a moment of "Ahhhh…" I know how to do this. This, I can control. This, I can navigate. This, I can rely on. As we heal from trauma, a daily ritual offers grounding, reliability, control, and comfort. Ritual helps us know that we continue. Doing this every day is a ceremony of self-compassion and healing.

Meditation:

Today, I rest in the arms of ritual. I have a daily ritual that is unique to me and my path. I perform my ritual mindfully, open to the healing it offers, grounding in the solid footing it provides me moving forward. I am thankful it offers me control in this moment. I am here, now. And I dedicate myself to be here tomorrow to once again take refuge and reassurance in this trusted space.

Today, I practice my ritual, grateful for the capacity I have to love myself through this daily practice. I breathe into the comfort of my ritual.

"Life is the ceremony. How we live it is the sacred ritual."
~ Wind Hughes

Journal prompt: Write out the details of a daily ritual you can employ. Describe the benefit of each aspect of the ritual. Give the ritual a name.

S

S = SELF-COMPASSION

*"Self-compassion is nurturing yourself with all the kindness
and love you would shower on someone you cherish."*
~ Debra L. Reble PhD

There is a reason self-compassion is so talked about in healing circles. It is because we are doing very hard work and we are deserving of compassion. Whether we have been in therapy, physical therapy, recovery, or any healing modality for trauma, ultimately, we must be our own healers. We employ tools we gather along the way, but we are the one in the trenches, slogging through and doing the work every single day. If that does not deserve compassion, what does? Even the Buddha is quoted as saying "If your compassion does not include yourself, it is incomplete."

Our natural tendency may be to judge ourselves and be self-critical, sometimes even of our own healing! We may question our methods, question our ability to cope, and beat ourselves up when we have a bad day. The invitation here is to notice when we slip into negativity, and find ways to offer compassion to yourself. This can be done by noticing how ready we are to offer compassion to others, to understand when they fall short, to support without question. Turning this same compassion toward ourselves can help us rise out of the quagmire of self-judgment, creating space so that our true self, our sense of loving awareness, can come forward and stand with us in our truth.

Meditation:

Today, I offer myself compassion. I imagine a trusted friend and I see them offer compassion to me. They are astonished at my healing and growth. They offer me nothing but love. I imagine myself as a child. I offer this child so much compassion and love. I wish this child peace for their journey and I have no judgement for this innocent child. I imagine myself in a mirror. I truly see the person I am, doing the best I can, and know that all I deserve today is compassion.

Today, I place my hand on my heart as a gesture of self-love. I feel comforted by this action and I breathe into the love it offers.

> *"Practice self-compassion. Talk to and BE your own best, kind, compassionate, caring friend."* ~ Kristin Neff

Journal prompt: Write a letter to yourself full of only love and compassion. Write the ways you are in awe of yourself (as a friend would be).

T

TRUST

"Sometimes we must break completely in order to rebuild fully. Trust your ability to transform." ~ Alex Elle

As a survivor of trauma, trust can be a major component in healing. It is difficult to restore trust when the stability we had before has been shaken from underneath us. It is natural to become hyper-vigilant and untrusting – of others, of God, and even of ourselves.

When we have experienced trauma, our sense of safety in the world is often absent. However, there is within us a drive, a human longing, to find those in whom we can trust. It can be a slow process, but every time you trust another soul, the trust will grow. Remember, you're trying to put back together a vase that has shattered into a hundred pieces. Joining two pieces is no small miracle. Take the time to put it back together at your own pace, with your own sense of comfort, but remain diligent!

When we feel we cannot trust God, we are at sea without a rudder, a sail, or an anchor. The mistaken thinking is that God somehow abandoned us in our trauma. Let me assure you, God never abandons us. Remember, when bad things happen, God is not in the event, God is in the response to the event. It is in those moments when we choose God that our Faith is strengthened, our Trust is emboldened, and our capacity for Love expands.

Meditation:

Today, I gather my hurt, fear, and sorrow into a bundle and place it in the arms of the Divine. I recognize I cannot live in a state of distrust. I breathe and acknowledge that restoring trust is a critical part of my healing. Living without trust in others, in myself, or in God is not sustainable. I look for situations and people that reinforce my belief in the goodness of life. I recall those people in my life who I can trust. I see the good and active choices I have made for my healing and know that I can trust myself.

Today, I choose to try trust. I turn my trust toward God and calm the stormy sea within.

"Recovery takes time to heal the heart, strengthen your confidence and find trust in yourself. In the end of your life it will be what you make of it, you get to write that chapter."
~ Tracy Malone

Journal prompt: Do you see areas where you are untrusting? Describe these areas and examine the validity of your feeling. Write what it would feel like to trust again in this area. What needs to happen for you to regain trust here?

U

UNBREAKABLE

"Your soul is unbreakable, no matter how broken it feels."
~ Samantha Camargo

Feeling broken as we heal from trauma is to be expected. We never thought our lives would be touched by trauma, and some days it's still hard to believe. We never thought we'd have to plumb the depths of what it means to be human, face the darkness of trauma, and then find ways to heal. Yet, here we are.

However, there is a place within us that is unbreakable, if only we can find it, focus on it, and spend time in that safe place.

Helen Keller, blind and deaf, wrote a poem about the loss of her sight, hearing and speech, ending it with this line regarding God: *"He would not let them take away my soul, possessing that I still possess the whole."* She had found that place inside her that was unbreakable, and knew that whatever befell her, whatever other losses she may go through, her soul remained intact. Whether we have been touched by trauma in our body or mind, our soul remains a solid vessel; affected yes, but not broken.

We can reach this holy place inside us by focusing within. Going within we find a conscious presence, a sense of loving awareness, that can only be touched by the Divine. It is whole, complete and unbreakable. It holds the vast knowledge of the universe and the small wonder of a child. It is a place of love and safety that is not broken and that is available to us as often as we choose to abide with it.

Meditation:

Today, I seek to dwell in the place inside of me that is unbreakable. I quiet my mind and breathe deeply, dropping down into a space within that is warm and soft and light-filled. I recognize my soul, the safety of my soul, and I rest here. As I breathe, my expanding breath feeds the light that is my soul until it fills my entire being. Though I have endured so much, by joining regularly with my spirit and with God, I know that truly, at the core of my being, I am unbreakable.

Today, I revel in the resilience of my spirit, the strength of God within me, and the solid touchstone that is my soul. I commit to carry this truth with me today. I am unbreakable.

> *"If they hadn't tried to break me down,*
> *I wouldn't know that I'm unbreakable."*
> ~ Gabourey Sidibe

Journal prompt: Meditate on the place in you that is unbreakable – then write from that place. How does it feel to tap into that core strength? What does your spirit want you to know?

V

V = VISION

"A vision is not just a picture of what could be; it is an appeal to our better selves, a call to become something more."
~ Rosabeth Moss Kanter

As we heal, it's helpful to hold a vision in our minds. Holding a vision of ourselves, whole and healed, crystallizes our daily work, giving us something tangible to strive for. This vision may shift as we heal, but the core essence of it will remain the same. We must be able to see a future in order to have one.

Imagine your future self. Imagine how you will live when you have fully integrated and healed trauma. Imagine how you will inhabit the world when you have alchemized trauma into an unstoppable fire in the belly. Hold this vision. See yourself as a warrior. See yourself as the victor. Trauma was not your choice, but you have not let it hold you back. You are whole again.

There are many tools for creating vision in your healing. You may hold a vision in your mind, write it down and journal about it, create a vision board and meditate on it daily. The important factor is to believe in your vision. Believe it is possible. Remember, so many others before you have healed trauma. So will you.

Meditation:

Today, I practice seeing in my mind's eye a vision of myself whole, healed, and at peace. I know my hard work has paid off and I see myself at peace and living a good life. I am proud of where I am in life.

Today, I hold this vision close to my heart, acknowledging how my heart, my soul, and my mind have all worked together to bring me to this point. I believe in my ability to bring this vision to life. I believe I will be healed. I believe God will walk this vision with me.

"When I dare to be powerful, to use my strength in the service of my vision – then it becomes less and less important whether I am afraid."
~ Audre Lorde

Journal prompt: Close your eyes and build a clear vision of your healed self. Write a description of yourself, add details about your feelings, attitudes, rituals, and surroundings. Spend some time in your vision.

W

WISDOM

"We don't receive wisdom; we must discover it for ourselves after a journey that no one can take for us or spare us."
~ Marcel Proust

Wisdom is hard won. Wisdom cannot be found in books or on the internet. Wisdom is that intangible state of knowing that only comes from life experience, from discerning thought, and deep reflection. When we are busy healing trauma, we are building bricks of wisdom. Even though we did not choose this, there is wisdom to glean from it, to carry forward with us.

As we heal trauma, we become wise in many aspects of life. We have wisdom in self-knowledge. We come to know how much we can carry, and what to let go. We grow wise in who to bring with us, and who to leave behind. We grow very wise in self-preservation, taking time for ourselves when needed, and joining with others in ways that feed our soul, not in ways that deplete us. We grow so wise in this alchemy! We take flashbacks, triggers, bad memories, rage, and hurt and transmute it into purposeful, useful, healing light. We grow wise enough to take the hand of others and help them up. Wisdom is hard won, and not to be taken lightly. Be grateful for all wisdom gained and yet to be gained.

Meditation:

Today, I center my thoughts on wisdom. I am grateful for the wisdom I have gained along my healing journey. I am grateful for the wisdom yet to come. I see that wisdom gained through pain is deeper than I could have ever imagined. It is a deep well I can draw from when I thirst for peace and safety. I trust myself to act and react from this place of wisdom, and see this beautiful glow of wisdom rooted in my solar plexus, growing and spreading throughout my being, radiant with self-confidence and faith.

Today, I rest in my own wisdom. I go forward in this day reliant on my wise, higher self.

"Meet me in the middle
of your story
when the soul
is worn
but wise."
~ Angie Weiland-Crosby

Journal prompt: Write about what you've learned about yourself on this healing journey. Describe what you have left behind and what wisdom you now carry. Who or what have you let go of that no longer served you?

X

X = (E)XERCISE

"Only exercise on the days you want to improve your mood."
~ Chalene Johnson

Regular exercise is critical to our physical health, of course. The benefits to our mental health are just as compelling. Exercise is a verified mood booster and it's incredibly helpful in healing trauma, as it helps our nervous system burn off adrenaline and releases endorphins. Endorphins, when they flood our nervous system, help us combat depression by actually reducing our perception of pain, thereby decreasing anxiety. Exercise can also help us feel in control of our bodies, and help us tune into the effect of stress on our physical well-being.

When we are at our lowest, it is often difficult to muster up the energy to exercise. These are actually the times it is most important. Getting yourself off the couch (or out of bed) and doing even light exercise increases our sense of resiliency. Trauma can leave our nervous system feeling vulnerable and incapable. Regular exercise can help us begin to rebuild our self-confidence and restore faith in our ability to take care of ourselves. Start with as much as you can handle, as with all healing tools, and build as you see the benefits. But do start!

Meditation:

Today, I commit to some form of exercise to benefit my mind and body. I rely on the strength of God to get me up and moving if I cannot find the strength myself. I honor myself by devoting time to exercise, seeing it as a gift to myself and my well-being. I am grateful to be alive, to be able to move my body in whatever way I can, in order to reduce any anxiety, stress, or depression in my system.

Today, as I exercise, I will be mindful of my heart beating in my chest, my breath cleansing my body, and my mind focusing on the present moment, clear and untroubled.

"Exercise is the key not only to physical health but to peace of mind."
~ Nelson Mandela

Journal prompt: What are your thoughts and feelings around exercise? Are you comfortable with it? Do you enjoy it or avoid it? Write a short check-in with yourself before and after exercising. How could your healing benefit from regular exercise?

Y

Y = YES

"Choose this life. Choose this body. Say yes to all of it. Say yes to the beauty and the good and the ugly and the difficult. Choose what you have, what you are. Choose this moment. Choose to love and remember. You are full. You are alive."
~ Kimber Simpkins

One aspect of healing trauma is learning to engage again with the world. Our initial response to trauma is often to withdraw and find safety within ourselves, or a trusted few people. This is absolutely normal and to be expected. As we heal, however, we need to tiptoe into society as it feels safe to do so. Social withdrawal and isolation can be a symptom of trauma that can delay our healing, and add to depression.

Venturing out to activities and places we once enjoyed can sometimes feel overwhelming. We may be exposed to triggers, or memories may surface that make us uncomfortable. We can only do as much as we can as we heal, but it is important that we keep trying. Saying "Yes" to life after trauma is not easy, but it does get easier over time, and only with practice. Have we been saying "No" and isolating? There is a time to cocoon as we heal, and there is a time to sidestep the draw of being alone, as it can feed depression if there is nothing to offset it. Ask God to walk with you as you venture out, and listen to the wisdom of your soul as you find your balance in saying "Yes."

Meditation:

Today, I imagine myself saying "Yes" to life. I examine those places or times in my life where perhaps I said "No" out of fear; fear of overwhelm, fear of feeling uncomfortable, or fear of lacking control of a situation. I soften around this fear, and offer myself loving compassion for these feelings, and love myself for doing the best I can on my healing journey.

Today, I commit to trying to say "Yes" more often, bringing trusted people with me, and finding a balance between my desire to avoid, and my desire to have connection. Today, I will attempt to trust life, trust myself, and trust God by saying "Yes."

"Say 'yes' to life! 'Yes' to wonder, to joy, to despair. 'Yes' to pain, 'yes' to what you don't understand. Try 'yes.' Try 'always.' Try 'possible.' Try 'hopeful.' Try 'I will.' And try 'I can.'"
~ Leo Buscaglia

Journal prompt: Are there places where I've been saying "no" to life? What would it take to say "yes?" Describe the areas you feel resistant to saying "yes" and examine what may lie underneath that.

Z

Z = ZEN

"Zen is a path of liberation. It liberates you. It is freedom from the first step to the last. You are not required to follow any rules; you are required to find out your own rules and your own life in the light of awareness." ~ Osho

The concept of Zen, although it comes from Buddhist practice and teachings, is also a noun describing a state of being. This state is that of a meditative calm, in which your inner wisdom is more available to you and can help guide your thoughts and actions. Our reliable gateway to enter this state is through the practice of meditation, mindfulness and prayer. These practices help us to stop shaking the snow globe of our mind and let the thoughts settle.

However, this is not the only way. Zen, in the traditional Buddhist sense, includes the cultivation of mentors and practicing in community. In this sense, striving toward a Zen mind touches upon very practical tools. Mentors help us see that we are not walking a new path, but one that is new for us, and they light luminarias that help us find our own way. Community helps us see we are not alone and that support is available for us, which brings us refuge and the ability to surrender. Mentors and community can both be found in therapeutic settings such as talk therapy or support groups. Meditation, mindfulness and prayer support our own innate ability to access our inner wisdom and heal our thoughts. Through these techniques, we actually rewire our mind to be able to bend more toward Zen in our daily lives.

Meditation:

Today, I seek a state of Zen consciousness, realizing true Zen takes many years of practice, but I will start today by breathing, regulating my breath, meditating and turning this trauma over to God. I trust God will ease my mind so I may find respite from struggle, and some moments of peace, tranquility and calm.

Today, I commit to nurturing myself by connecting with mentors and others who can help me deepen my practice, whether through meditation, yoga, prayer, or therapy. I trust that the tools I use and am drawn to will work together so I may experience glimpses of my Zen mind, already within me, simply waiting for me to enter the gate.

"Zen is not effort. Effort is tension, effort is work, effort is to achieve something. Zen is not something to achieve. You are already that. Just relax, relax so deeply you become a revelation to yourself."
~ Zen teaching

Journal prompt: Write about the mentors in your life. Who are the wise ones you can look to for guidance? What is the community in which you find support and connection? Describe a Zen moment, either real or imagined. What are the ingredients of that moment?

IN APPRECIATION

I have many people to thank for inspiring, reading, proofreading, and encouraging this project!

My sister, Peggy Holmes, for showing me what resilience and healing after trauma looks like, and helping me know it was possible for me too. I miss you every day, but am so grateful that you were my sister, and continue to be, in spirit.

My lifelong chosen sisters, Gail Andrews and Mimi O'Connor, whose strength and wisdom have been the rudder on my lifeboat for most of my life! Thank you for your steadfast love and friendship and for holding me up and for so much laughter through many tears!

My husband, William Hubbard, for being my safe harbor, my anchor at times, and for giving me the space and time for these deep thoughts, deep healing, and creative process.

My son, Trevor Lebsock, for always encouraging my creative projects, and for being a sounding board and inspiration for healing.

My mother, Juanita McGee, for the gift of writing. My father, George McGee, for the gift of deep faith.

Several therapists and spiritual counsel over the years, because it's a process! Your gentle wisdom and guidance were always exactly what I needed at exactly the right time. My many students over the span of my career. Often, helping you walk through trauma, you taught me more than you know.

My highest thanks goes to God for walking every step of healing with me. I invited, and you came, and you stayed, and have never abandoned me. Beyond that, God gave me these thoughts and these words and now I give it to you.

ABOUT THE AUTHOR

Victoria McGee is a spiritual writer, focusing on the healing of trauma. Her blog, Still Beloved, is a source of healing for many on the journey of trauma recovery. She lives in Ventura County, California with her husband, 2 dogs, 2 cats, and 8 chickens.

stillbeloved.com

victoriamcgee.com